medicate them into submission

david rogers

A Collection of Song Lyrics
by David Rogers

"Red for passion, desire and love.
Blue for wisdom and faith."
Oh Marisela c.07/2017

"There's no explainin' the words in my brain
They just come spillin' out of me
Prone to the spurious epiphany
A twisted poet at the turn of the century."
Twisted Poet c.06/2015

1981-1998

Copyright © 2020 LogomanMusic
logomanmusic@gmail.com

Table of Contents

What's Wrong with America? 1
Moxie 2
Summer's Leaving Town 3
Ain't Gonna Get Mad 4
Big Blue River 5
Quick Love 6
Short Porch to Right 7
You Know That I Will 8
More Than I Deserve 9
Likely Story 10
Noche Perdida 11
Blues Today 12
Kittybone 13
One Angry Survivor 14
Pretty Young Thing 15
Shindy 16
The Undertaker 17
Hale-Bopp Boogie 18
Lick My Chops 19
That Voodoo 20
What Is Love? 21
Stop Doggin' Me 22
Shivaree 23
Moments Worth Living For 24
Short-Lived Glory 25
Tipple Tonight 26
Avarice 27
No Easy Way Home 28
Bluegrass and Rye 29
Out on the Levee Road 30
Hoot n' Holler 31
Yer Poor Mama 32
Victory Without Reward 33
Schmidt 34
Brother Joe 35
Medicate Them Into Submission 36

Ev'ry Dawg	37
Fifty-Three	38
Chest of Drawers	39
Just Like Valerie Nash	40
Wake Up Dead	41
Just in Time for Havana	42
House on Fire	43
Skunk on a Hill	44
Barnacle on a Rock	45
Fountains of Fire	46
Calavera	47
Back in '39	48
Hottie Down the Hall	49
This Is My Only Life	50
Purblind Boys	51
Destruction Addiction	52
Twisted Poet	53
Jerk	54
Clean and Jerk	55
Slums of Columbus	56
Condemn Nation	57
Right Side of the Law	58
Bad Consumer	59
Come on, October	60
Georgia, Bold and Black	61
Sorry, Sweetheart	62
Trophy Shelf	63
Cherry Aurora	64
Billet-Doux for You	65
Deadman's Hill	66
King of Cuba	67
My Anodyne	68
Last Laugh	69
Love to Do	70
Heat of July	71
Oh! Marisela	72
Justice Has Left the Building	73
Persona	74

B-Cup Beauty Queen 75
Perihelion 76
Disorder Syndrome 77
Finger in It..78
I Predicted Pain 79
Halfway to First..80
Today in the Park 81
Just Like Buck 82
Nothing is Sacred 83
Roaring 20's 84
Cupid Sneaks In 85
She Came in Peace 86
First to Fall 87
Take a Day..88
Twenty-Second Century.. 89
Guardian Angel 90
The Potter's Field 91
La Perla.. 92

What's Wrong with America?

The curtain opened like a giant eyelid
But there was nobody standing behind it
Seduced by a job with a better wage
It was a full house playing to an empty stage
I remember the moment when I first heard the news
It was a situation they could not refuse
But you can never ever really leave the game
Ain't that what all them old ballplayers say
Selling twenty room mansions that they just bought
There's never enough room at the top
Yesterday I felt so good and everything was fine
I should've recognized the warning sign
In the church choir at Saint Elizabeth's school
All the little girls and boys were dressed in blue
Holding hands, they sang a sad little song
America the beautiful, what is wrong?
What's wrong with America?

Moxie

She got the moxie, she ain't backin' down

She got the moxie, baby, she gonna stand her ground

It takes more work than I ever imagined

This ain't workin' out quite like I planned it

And you ain't savin' nothin' for a rainy day

You know what they say

You can't get somethin' for nothin' baby

She got the moxie, I gotta get me some

She got the moxie baby, and I ain't got none

Sound of breaking glass up on the 14th floor

The suit that lived above me couldn't take no more

And the final taxi…it only got one destination

The cause of death; defenestration

You got the moxie, I gotta get me some

You got the moxie baby, and I ain't got none

I got a razor down beside my bed

Revolver in the nightstand drawer

Deadbolts all up and down my door

You say, what you need all that hardware for?

I got the moxie, gonna stand my ground

I got the moxie, baby, I ain't backin' down

Summer's Leaving Town

Summer is leaving town
Taking with her the last of the sunny days
Moving without a sound
Oh, you know she's always been that way
Sailing into a cool breeze
Never turning around to say goodbye
The scenery has me surrounded
This wilderness is beginning to bring me down
Gonna head for the horizon and disappear
Between the ground and the clear blue sky
Summer is leaving town
A classic beauty in a state of disrepair
Nothing pending now except the ending
To another meaningless affair

Ain't Gonna Get Mad

I ain't gonna get mad, I ain't gonna get even
I'm gonna get me a ticket on the next train
The next train leaving
Wherever I'm going is better than where I been
I was a fool but it ain't gonna happen again
She tore my playhouse down
The first night I met her
She gonna run back home to her mama
Every time I upset her
I tell you, boys, this time I ain't goin' to get her
She said please baby
Can you meet me when the sun goes down
I been standin' right here all night
Waitin' for that girl to come around

Big Blue River

From Springfield to Sutter's fort
Head straight for the setting sun
With an emigrant's guide and a Christian bible
A pike and a loaded gun
500 wagons rolled out of Missouri
'Twas for the wilderness they departed
There ain't no reason to worry, they heard
It gets easier once you get started
Ferry me over the big blue river
Carry me into the Kansas plain
Remember to never take no cutoff
And hurry along just as fast as you can
Four days crossing a 40-mile desert
And 400 miles to go
Freezing cold in the canyons
In the mountains it's starting to snow
I pray that I live to see California
To be with my family and friends
Remember to always do the best that you can
If I should never see you again

Quick Love

What is it that fuels the attraction?

I'm trying to decide

It's almost five in the morning

She hums a sweet little song

As I go back and forth

Back and forth like Gunga Din to satisfy our thirst

Watching intently as a drop of water runs a course

Over her chin and down her neck

Through beads of sweat

And each time is better yet

Than the one that came before it

Enraptured by the way her fingers dance and play

The way she crawls across the floor

Bella fica, bella fica it is just like a dream

Can we stop this moment in time between

The dark of night and the breaking of dawn?

There is no choice but to go on from here

How and where will we take it?

This quick love

Short Porch to Right

Opening day in the year 2000
Out on the mound completely surrounded
In the first game that was ever played
On the field of dreams by the edge of the bay
That field of dreams was a beautiful sight
More than 40 grand packed in tight
339 down the left field line and a short porch to right
Make some noise for the boys of summer
The black and orange are puttin' up a crooked number
In the first game that was ever played
On the field of dreams by the edge of the bay
That field of dreams was an emerald green
40,000 fans screamin' for the home team
339 down the left field line and a short porch to right
Ninth inning and the game was tied
Pinch-hitting lefty sees a fastball inside
In the first game that was ever played
On the field of dreams by the edge of the bay

You Know That I Will

What's the matter with you, baby?

You been actin' pretty strange

Said you got something real important to tell me

So why you keep on stayin' away

You make it all look so easy

Just turn around and walk the other way

Now that I see where you're comin' from

Honey I will meet you halfway

You know that I will, darlin' you know I will

You know that I will

'Cause I will do anything for your love

I'm gonna keep fixin' my broken-up heart

Every time you leave it black and blue

And the very next time that I see you, girl

I'm gonna give it right back to you

You know that I will, darlin' you know I will

You know that I will

'Cause I will do anything for your love

And I will forgive you, yes I will

I will forgive you, you know that I will

More Than I Deserve

Sometimes I get more than I deserve

Surrounded such as I am

By the trappings which confine me

And time does not stand still

Oh no, far from it

And it's time, time that I got started

Am I going nowhere or everywhere all at once?

Is it all too much or never quite enough?

A few good friends are still hanging tough

Waiting for me to decide

Sometimes I get more than I deserve

And I'm so restless all of the time

Can't seem to locate the middle ground

Take a long last look around

Before you begin to forget

The life of the party will be the death of me yet

Likely Story

She's a likely story
Racing against the clock
Holding out for quite some time now
Holding on to what she's got
The dividends for one lucky winner
The goods to be delivered
You talk about a master plan
I'm talkin' 'bout love and romance
She's like a tonic for depression
If you'll pardon my expression
Absolutely sweet and true
If they only knew, if they only knew
She's a likely story
In possession of a singular style
Mixing in a little mystery
To keep them guessing for awhile
Patience is the art of waiting
Youth is the frame of mind
Faith is the abstract painting
Truth is the glass of wine

Noche Perdida

Open up the window and close your eyes

Can you feel the temperature rise?

Aji dulce, you're as hot as you are sweet

Bocachera in the square and samba in the street

Let the rhythm of the music make you feel all right

Just like Lalo up in Spanish Harlem

Gonna fill you up with pride

Just gimme a little kiss at midnight, señorita

This is the beginning of the noche perdida

Blues Today

It was a very difficult year

Kept reminding us that nothing is permanent here

Things could get better, they could get worse

Never seems to stay the same just when you want it to

And I don't believe you know

How much you did for me, my friend

Now I can only hope that you're back in the wind again

This is not the way that I wanted to say goodbye

And that's the reason why I got the blues today

This life is a funny thing

Keeps us busy and tries to make us forget

It will put the miles between us

And try to pull us apart

Half the time makin' us hurry

And half the time makin' us wait

And now it's too late, it's out of my hands

Guess it's one of those things I'll never understand

This is not the way that I wanted to say goodbye

And that's the reason why I got the blues today

Kittybone

Oh girl yer makin' me crazy
Some of the things you say
Ooh girl ya make me so nervous
When you lookin' at me that way
We're cuttin' out the middleman
From the vine right into the frying pan
Oh girl yer makin' me crazy
Some of the things you do
Ooh girl ya make me so nervous
Whenever I get next to you
Way better than a cooking show
I'll take either one or both of those
Right up to 117
The way big love was meant to be
Better than a numbers game
Gimme nothing less than more of the same
Now I'm really up against it
And I think it's beginning to show
Now we really got it goin' on
Gettin' down with kittybone

One Angry Survivor

One angry survivor

Who will take almost anything you have to give

Who will wait impatiently for a package

That cannot be delivered

Fatalism or clairvoyance

The implications were profound

Exactly one half year to build it up together

Only fifteen minutes to tear it down

Communication in a straight line

Sensational sound and light

Come to understand it better

Always very late at night

Eloquence and instant wisdom

The declarations were so proud

Exactly one half year to build it up together

Only fifteen minutes to tear it down

Pretty Young Thing

Ain't much to look at

I mean look at the shape I'm in

Got nothing to call my own

I been scuffling for so long

Shut out for years

Gettin' sick and tired of it all

I'm sick of it here and I'm tired of living alone

I'm so tired of living alone

They say there's someone for everyone

Won't some pretty young thing come on and love me

Ain't nothin' to brag about

But you know you could do worse in this town

Like something left at the lost and found

Wearing thin but I'm not worn out

They say there's someone for everyone

Won't some pretty young thing come on and love me

Shindy

Almost killed myself again last night
I'm an accident waiting to happen
What was I thinking about
While I was getting out of my head
No stopping for the sake of sanity
Careening through the break of dawn
What's up with all this carrying on?
That shindy just keeps rolling along
Did I remember to return the call?
Did I give them my regards?
Did I put my past back up on the shelf?
Is the future still on hold?
For a minute or two I thought that I was someone else
But I'm just another careless fool
Who lives to forgive and forget
I know that I'm going down
I guess my number hasn't come up yet

The Undertaker

A word to the wise

I've seen the same look in a thousand eyes

It's the wisdom of the ages

Spoken by sages for so many years

Give me your tired, give me your weary

I will take it from here

Give me your tired, give me your weary

I know just how it feels

I'm right next to the next of kin

You're on your way to meet your maker

I've done this very thing so many times before

I am the undertaker

Hale-Bopp Boogie

Big production goin' on in space
Heavenly bodies all over the place
Quasars sendin' out radio waves
It's the show that never stops
Perseid meteors runnin' their course
Big red giants and little white dwarfs
Supernovas brighter than a galaxy
It's the show that never stops
Hale-bopp, hale-bopp
The show that never stops
Shannon Lucid is passin' by
A point of light movin' in a straight line
Vega climbin' up the eastern sky
It's the show that never stops
Stars that blast themselves to pieces
Stars that simply fade away
Stars that slowly come apart
It's the show that never stops
Hale-bopp, hale-bopp
The show that never stops

Lick My Chops

Mama got a face like a bulldog

Papa's gettin' paid to play ball

Sissy got a leg up on the action

And Junior's in trouble with the law

The suits are in a frenzy like never before

And they're all jacked into the grid

It's business as usual at the watering hole

Sometimes hot, sometimes cold

The city's gettin' meaner by the minute

Every mother's son is packin' heat

Maybe the workin' girls down by the precinct

Will give the deputies a little treat

She was over the hill, a street-walkin' girl

But man, she had a big jug o' wine

I'm here to say, about six drinks later

That ol' girl was lookin' fine

Now Junior got a job in distribution

Real friendly with the local cops

Sissy's out lookin' for a good time

The tricks are all lickin' their chops

That Voodoo

Goin' back to Harlem, gotta start all over again

Took a turn for the worse out in California

Almost drove me over the edge

Shreveport, Louisiana by way of New Orleans

Stoppin' for a little while at all points in between

Lord, out in Kansas City I did gamble and I did sin

You know I lost everything I had

When I first rolled in

Went out to see the ponies, puttin' on a little parlay

Me and Voodoo was sittin' pretty

'Til some bugboy got in the way

The eloquent jive, the signifyin'

Truth be told she got a heart of gold

That ain't even the half of it yet

That Voodoo, she 'bout as funky as a girl can get

What Is Love?

What is love? What is love?
Is it something you can have for free?
Is it something that you can see?
What is love? What is love?
Is it quiet or is it loud?
Is it lighter than a cloud?
I've heard that love will make you richer
I've heard that love will make you poorer
I'm just trying to figure it out
Does anybody know what they're talkin' about?
What is love? What is love?
Can you get it from somebody else?
Can you keep it all to yourself?
I've heard that love will make you weaker
I've heard that love will make you stronger
I'm just trying to figure it out
Does anybody know what they're talkin' about?
What is love? What is love?

Stop Doggin' Me

Stop doggin' me, baby
You're barking up the wrong tree
Sniffing all around like a bloodhound
You're always doggin' me
Stay out of the way
Girl, go out and have some fun
If you keep on interrupting me
This song ain't never gonna get done
Now baby, what you cryin' about?
You know everything is gonna work out fine
Remember what I said when we first got together
I said I'd always treat you right
So quit pushin' me baby
I'm moving just as fast as I can
And stop condescending
'Cause darlin', I understand

Shivaree

Yessiree boys

Now that's what I call a real fine shivaree

I was crooked for two straight days

Or maybe it was three

I ain't never been invited to no highbrow occasion

I ain't none too familiar with no fancy places

Gonna have to muster up all of my social graces

Me and a debutante was dancin' a minuet

She was the sweetest little pippin I have ever met

Throw out the book of rules

I'll just play this one by ear

All the young ladies are hiding my number

Whenever I come near

I was playin' me some three card monte

Winnin' two out of every three

A coureur de bois and a cousin jenny

Their gold dust was comin' to me

Jimmy Jack was the mustard king

He come and save the day

Bought up everything we had to sell

And gave it back for free

Moments Worth Living For

It's another fine mess I've left behind

In the selfish pursuit of a new situation

If only I had the nerve

To keep on going and never look back

Well I know myself a little better than that

There can be no graceful exit

There will be no peaceful journey

Across this rugged landscape

This minefield I call my mind

The crying waitress is coming apart

Wailing like a siren winding down

Pieces of her shattered heart lying all around

The pumping blood begins to flow

So painful, so unintentional

It was as far as I could go

And the moments worth living for

Lay scattered and brushed aside

Innocent and unattended

Like victims at the scene of a crime

Short-Lived Glory

If it's alright with you, then baby, it's alright with me

I don't give a damn about my reputation

Double shot of envy and a dram of admiration

What's a mystery to me is so obvious to you

Short-lived glory, end of story

Or the start of something new

Otherwise occupied, presently indisposed

It so happens I'm fresh out of self-discipline

Washing down vitamins with the last of the gin

And the crying waitress...

Was it a place we used to go

Or someone I used to know?

Tipple Tonight

Quarter to four and my telephone's ringin'
I don't mind at all
Ya make my heart feel like singin'
Anytime i get your call
Yeh you ripe for the pickin'
Like a time bomb tickin'
Got every little thing i like
Ya make me feel alright
Come on pretty baby, we gonna tipple tonight
Gonna tell you what's on my mind
Only wanna hold you all of the time
Someday babe, you gonna acquiesce
And put my sweet love to the test
Come on pretty baby, we gonna tipple tonight

Avarice

There's so much I don't want to remember

There are some things I will never forget

To fall in love with a fascinating woman

To look at her face

Listen to the sound of her voice

Accessible pleasures I would never deny

And I'll admit to committing carnal sins

But I will not confess to a crime

Vanity and lust will thrive

In such a vulnerable situation

I was decidedly guilty of avarice

For want of reciprocation

The final act was a pitiful performance

Recognize it for what it was

Truly decadent theater

The tenuous trust, barely alive

Amidst all the deprivation

Now silenced by the decision you have made

No Easy Way Home

There's plenty of victims on the highway

And half of them are going my way

If I can just blend in with the pack

I think I can make it back to safety

But the future never looks too bright

For the last horse out the gate

The promise of sweet victory

Is already running late

Straight lines and curves

And clever plays on words

Somebody else's design

Is gonna get you every time

Speeding past the warning signs

Driving on the wrong side of the road

I got news for ya, baby

There ain't no easy way home

Bluegrass and Rye

Just give me something I can believe in
Just give me someone I can trust
Old time tradition is what brings us all together
Gives everybody time for a little break
Seventh inning stretch on the fourth of July
Fireworks are lightin' up the sky
Have you ever seen anything more beautiful in your life
Would you look at all that bluegrass and rye
Faith is my protector in this city
Where it's hard to tell the sinners from the saints
I've always been at ease in the company of strangers
Now they're tellin' me it can never be the same
Seventh inning stretch on the fourth of July
Fireworks are lightin' up the sky
Have you ever seen anything more beautiful in your life
Would you look at all that bluegrass and rye

Out on the Levee Road

Out on the levee road

Seems like time is standing still

Seems like it's always grey and cold

And I'm walking all alone

Way out on the levee road

Out on the levee road

Tried walkin' off these blues

But the pouring rain fills up my shoes

And my passway is full of stones

Way out on the levee road

Now if I had me an automobile

I could ride right up the causeway

Roll straight in to the center of town

But I spent my last dollar bill

A long long while ago

Now I spend all my time, all my time

Way out on the levee road

Hoot n' Holler

I went down to the junction
Just to see what was goin' on
Some kind of a social function
They gonna hoot n' holler all day long
I went down to the juke joint
Just to see what was goin' on
Corn liquor flowin', a jug band blowin'
They gonna hoot n' holler all night long
Well I was on my way to see my sweet Marie
Glory be, that girl was waitin' on me
How lucky can one fella be
Went past the house of ill repute
Just to see what was goin' on
Some skinny little dude had him a big fat mama
She got the chicken shakin' on her bones
Two blind pigs down on Picayune Street
You know there's always somethin' going on
They got the gospel and blues, they got the canned heat
They gonna hoot n' holler all night long

Yer Poor Mama

Good God Almighty child
Ain't you never gonna settle down
When you ever gonna ease on up
Runnin' crazy all over this town
What you tryin' to do to yourself
You know it can't be good for your health
Lord only knows why you actin' this way
Ain't that what yer poor mama would say
You a frisky little colt, you a real high stepper
Got the spike heel shoes and the lowneck sweater
Likin' hot new items and sweet sticky things
Puttin' that chili sauce on them chicken wings
Right now you really cuttin' loose
Struttin' all around with that fine caboose
Someday child you gonna have to pay
Ain't that what yer poor mama would say

Victory Without Reward

Standing in line

Starting to run out of time

My life keeps flashing before my eyes

But I know that I'm not dying

Maybe it's my imagination

Maybe it's nothing at all

Hope I don't keep you waiting

Hope I don't let you down

Seems like I'm always in a hurry

Feeling like I'll never arrive

There's no way to go straight ahead

And no way around the side

Trying to give something back to you

Trying to do the best that I can

But now that you're not here anymore

Who am I doing this for?

Schmidt

I don't want to be like Schmidt

Just planted by the side of the road

Mortal souls movin' on past

The nondescript epitaph

I don't want to be like that

Don't give me no tombstone

Just give me a bench in a park

A love of man, a fear of God

Parochial, patriarch

Just put it on a bench in a park

I don't want to be like Schmidt

Just planted by the side of the road

No claim to fame, no sobriquets

Them wooden crosses and cheap bouquets

I don't want to be like that

I don't wanna be like Schmidt

Brother Joe

Traveling north on interstate five
Leaning out the window on the passenger side
Tossed my cookies, lost my pride
I was heaving down life's highway
Bought some property in a pleasant town
Got a loyal wife and a faithful hound
Self-medicatin' and self-employed
I'm livin' off the interest of what I owe
Brother Joe...
One man's ceiling is another man's floor
Ask me how come and I'll tell you what for
What I see might not be what you heard
My sharp nine could be your minor third
Brother Joe...
Whoa my nightmare is every man's dream
Two chicks ain't always what it seems
369 down on the hardwood floor
Then me and Woody, we was out the door
Brother Joe...

Medicate Them Into Submission

They say the victim was from out of town

The pills and booze is what brought him down

Tried to fit the key into every door

Finally made it into room 24

Put the silencer on a revolver

And shot himself in the head

It wasn't 'til two days later

They finally found him dead

With the silence comes the pressure

With the darkness comes the pulse

There's nothing at all on the tv screen

And no one else here but the ghost and me

Medicate them into submission

And maybe they'll fix themselves

Prescription pills with free refills

Beware of the cure that kills

Magical mythical places

Smiles upon everyone's faces

The inner demons are lurking around

Ready to drag you down

Ev'ry Dawg

There were beautiful faces, yes, and a groovy beat

Them people were really dancin'

Me, I was just moving my feet

Now I'm waitin' in a queue but that's ok

'Cause ev'ry dawg has his day

Down in the south of France they was doin' a shoot

Brigitte Bardot wearin' her birthday suit

Ya know they got their ducks all in a row

And havin' them a faix do do

A bluestocking and a flim-flam man

Like Audrey Hepburn and Cary Grant

She quick with the lip, full of quotes and quips

He shootin' it straight right from the hip

A French poodle or a freakin' Great Dane

Ev'ry dawg has his day

Walkin' down the street in my business attire

Shakin' my booty to the Baptist choir

If it feels good do it that's all I'm sayin'

'Cause ev'ry dawg has his day

Fifty-Three

I'm loving life, I'm living large

Feeling hale and hearty

Yeh my life is kinda like one big long cocktail party

53 and doing fine, 53 hey my number's prime

Got no pills to take, no stress or strain

I don't worry 'bout any damn thing

No secrets to keep, no promises to break

And I ain't got no confessions to make

No debts to pay, no alimony

Laissez les bon temps roulet

No bones to pick, no butts to kick

No crosses to bear and I got all my hair

53 and doing fine, 53 hey my number's prime

Chest of Drawers

I'm tired of foolin' around with loose women and whores

Now it's time to find me a true fine love

But she got to have a chest of drawers

I been to the junior prom

I been to the antique stores

Now it's time for me to go shoppin'

For a girl with a chest of drawers

The Dorito chip, the landing strip

I seen all that stuff before

Now it's time for me to jump on top

Of a girl with a chest of drawers

I been to the Asian market, I been to the mental ward

Now I don't care about her state of mind

She just got to have a chest of drawers

I promise to love her from this day forward

And I pray thee to have and hold

I will worship at her tabernacle

But there best be a chest of drawers

Just Like Valerie Nash

There's hundreds of ways to take your life
But nothing quite so brash
As to take a chainsaw to your own neck
Just like Valerie Nash
They found her in a queen-size bed
Her favorite color crimson red
Maybe that's what made Valerie decide
On such a bloody suicide
It takes a certain…je ne sais quoi
To select above all…a chainsaw
It takes a strong constitution
Methode nonpareil…absolution
Valerie Nash, Valerie, Valerie Nash
The note that Mr. Bang left was stark
He said I am tormented by my debts
So he locked himself inside of his car
And fired up the charcoal briquettes

Wake Up Dead

I can get a date any old time
My little black book is doin' just fine
But I can't commit to no steady thing
'Cause I'm still wearin' that wedding ring
My pulse is racing and that ain't all
I got a buzz in my head from all that alcohol
Should've gone home but I'm out doggin' instead
One of these days I'm gonna wake up dead
Oh yeh I saw you just yesterday
Turned around and watched you walkin' away
You're way too hot to be left all alone
Let me help you girl, let me take you home

Just in Time for Havana

A young woman stands contemplating the sea
One part indifference, one part introspection
At least that's how it seemed to me
Waves roll in and ease back out
Some twice the size of others
And the moon moves the tides
Yes, the moon moves the inner soul
Climbing up the side of a forty-foot swell
Riding like Teddy up San Juan Hill
Phyrric victories, bitter defeat
Social injustice and indecency
Penitence paid, my peace is found
My physical strength has come around
Just in time, Lord, just in time for Havana

House on Fire

Have mercy on the wicked designs

Of your brothers and sisters

Hold your thunder

Don't carry no grudge in your arsenal

Let no man or beast trample you asunder

And when deliverance comes like a gun to your head

Turn around and run the other way

Like the house was on fire

Have pity on all the shitty little liars and signifiers

Walk that dividing line like a cat on a fence

Don't you know the time has come

To quit the scenes of your youth

So steel your resolve like the edge of a knife

And then turn around and run the other way

Like the house was on fire

Skunk on a Hill

Something around here is beautiful

But it ain't lookin' back from the mirror

Something around here is organized

But it ain't nothin' sent from above

Something around here is suspicious

But it ain't comin' from the golden temple

Something around here is outrageous

But I ain't talkin' 'bout the LGBT

Something here doesn't smell too good

Maybe it's coming from the skunk on a hill

Someone around here's doing time

For fighting racism, poverty and crime

Someone 'round here is painting pictures

About as clear as Picasso or Monet

Someone here is sending out signals

But they don't have a thing to say

Someone 'round here is singin' lullabies

Hopin' the children will sleep at night

Something here doesn't smell too good

Maybe it's coming from the skunk on a hill

Barnacle on a Rock

Hold on tight I say

Like a barnacle on a rock

You ain't seen nothin' yet

Get ready for the aftershock

Wait to be served I say

Like a barnacle on a rock

Something comes in on a wave

Absolutely ad hoc

Fuck or be fucked I say

Like a barnacle on a rock

The government and big business

Screwin' us around the clock

Live and let live I say

Like a barnacle on a rock

Let's get the party started

Looks like it's beer o'clock

Fountains of Fire

I see fountains of fire

And the flames are growing higher

Something's gone terribly wrong

The forces of nature will not be denied

And lightning will strike you twice

If you stay in one place for too long

The raging river may carry you home

It may carry you to your death

The rushing wind may speed your journey

It may take away your breath

This is not a painting, this is real life

This is not a work of art

This is the time and place

Where we start all over again

This is real life

Calavera

I went out to St. Louis
To see if I could have me some fun
Ain't nobody got no money out there
But everybody's carryin' a gun
Got to sleep down in a doorway
To get some shelter from the cold
Got my right hand on my razor
Yeh, to keep from gettin' rolled
You know I'm wearin' my calavera
On a chain right around my neck
There sure ain't no police 'round about here
Gonna serve, defend or protect

Back in '39

Back in '39 when swing was all the rage

No one could compare to Basie, Jones and Page

My father saw my mother standing all alone

They began to jitterbug and then he took her home

Six in the morning, the sky is still dark

Wish I could just go back to bed

Gotta be on my feet from 8 until 5

You know I'd rather be sleeping instead

Sitting on the steps out in front of my flat

Watching all the people walkin' by

Listening to the sounds of my neighborhood

I'd make a joyful noise if I only could

Hottie Down the Hall

The click of the heels, the click of the lock
Seventeen stories made of cinderblock
The long freight train movin' real slow
200 bicycles and one bateau
The sound of piano and a mandolin
Somebody's learnin' how to play the violin
The Jewish couple are havin' a fight
Somethin' above me goin' bump in the night
The pizza parlor, the hamburger joint
The massage parlor with a cash point
A view from the top and a hottie down the hall
An old coyote livin' on the hill
A blind man lookin' for a sleeping pill
Russian girls come to see the English bloke
Stairwell smellin' of medicinal smoke
Laundry room full of Mexican maids
And life goes on behind the shades
A view from the top and a hottie down the hall

This Is My Only Life

This is my only life

Please don't take it away from me

Erase all the lines on the map of the world

Well, well, well, and set me free

It's 120 in the desert

But we don't care 'cause we're not there

And where we are it's all very nice

Well, well, well, ain't we livin' in paradise

Now we cut to the hot weathergirls

Laughing, smiling as the violence unfurls

And now back to more pain and misery

Well, well, well, this is prime time tv

This is my only life

Please don't take it away from me

Purblind Boys

Round up the purblind boys
And send them off to war
Who needs the Geneva Convention
No one heeds that shit no more
Round up the purblind boys
And send them off to die
Who gives a fuck anymore
About the treaty of Versailles
Round up the purblind boys
And send them overseas
United we stand, a capital plan
Force-feeding democracies
Who needs to talk when we can shoot one another
Peace and love to ya, brother
Round up the last of the Romans
Who loved their enemy and killed their neighbor
Why glorify the founding fathers
Owners of persons in service and labor
"The passing of time shows that
Everything belongs to the future
And the conquerors will die
More surely than the conquered"

Destruction Addiction

Feel free to start anytime
The hard part is to not lose your way
And to not make the same mistakes twice
It was not my true nature to be very nice
This is all beautiful is what I'd like to say
But it's not my style to let my emotions betray
The way that I really feel
Oh yes, destruction addiction is real
I thought I saw these things in a movie
But it wasn't a movie, no, it was my life
It cost me everything that ever mattered
Lost my children, lost my wife
I'm used to using lies and alibis
To conceal the way that I really feel
So if I could just break the silence
I can tell you destruction addiction is real

Twisted Poet

A saxophone solo in the dead of night
Anarchist out lookin' for a reason to fight
There's just too much peace and not enough war
And the patriots are in an uproar
Someone better leave the security lights on
So the fighter pilot knows where to drop the bomb
Is it burn down the village, rebuild the town
Construction before destruction
Or the other way around?
There's no explainin' the words in my brain
They just come spillin' out of me
Prone to the spurious epiphany
A twisted poet at the turn of the century
While standing in line down at the zpg
An officer of the peace started barkin' at me
Put your hands in the air, turn around and freeze
I couldn't do it, it was 102 degrees

Jerk

Bought a six of ale and some cheap cabernet
With a counterfeit twenty I made yesterday
Went by the five and dime, said hi to the gents
Stole a couple items, spent forty cents
Called my wife from a payphone
Said the car broke down
Now I'm off to see my girlfriend way across town
I'm a lyin' cheatin' moneychangin'
Shopliftin' jerk
I said how ya doin' toots
And slapped her big behind
Went straight to the cupboard
To see what I could find
Mixed me up a drink and took me a seat
Told the sidedish to fix me somethin' to eat
Called up my boss, said I had some kinda bug
Ten minutes later we was cuttin' a rug
I'm a lyin' cheatin' moneychangin'
Shopliftin' jerk

Clean and Jerk

The churning mass of bones and flesh
It just would not give way
The art of Fred Astaire was lost
Somewhere in that vulgar display
And no one here is gonna do you a favor
They're ratcheting up the bad behavior
Two bon mots and one cheap shot
It's getting pretty cold in the melting pot
That woman over there never meant nobody harm
Her old man died with a needle in his arm
Ain't it a shame when you're livin' on the street
Got nothin' to drink, got nothin' to eat
You lose some friends, you win some bets
Strung out, strung up like marionettes
Take a good look at your handiwork
And say goodbye to the clean and jerk

Slums of Columbus

At long last there is peace in the castle

We quarreled and cussed and thought we must part

But now we've come crawling back

Back into each other's hearts

I have no plans for the summer

Other than the sun and some waves

And I am still here in the slums of Columbus

Living the life of a libertine

I once was enamored of psychology

I guess it's fair to say I was a shrink wannabe

Then I stopped caring about other people's drama

And started taking care of my own

Happy is happy and sad is sad

It ain't the same thing as good and bad

And I am still here in the slums of Columbus

Living the life of a libertine

Condemn Nation

Ain't got no syndromes or disorders that I can see

But that face lookin' back from the mirror...

Man, that can't be me

I need some medicinal weed for anxiety

Anxiety caused by not having any more weed

What ya gonna do when ignorance ruins you?

What ya gonna do when innocence won't protect you?

I'm not gonna ask you any questions

And I don't care about the reason why

I don't initiate conversation, I only reply

I'm kinda like Georgie Porgie

Kiss the girls and make them cry

What ya gonna do when ignorance ruins you?

What ya gonna do when innocence won't protect you?

The communist manifesto

And the constitution of the United States

They both have some pretty good information

But I succeed not because of thee but in spite of thee

My country...the condemn nation

Right Side of the Law

It's a pretty strange place to be
And it's all kind of new to me
After years of going wrong
I'm on the right side of the law
Now I got a family
And they're all depending on me
After years of going wrong
I'm on the right side, the right side of the law
The wind comes whisperin' through the trees
It's a breath of life, it's a cool, cool breeze
And this ain't even as good as it gets
God's gonna make a man out of me yet
After years of going wrong
I'm finally on the right side of the law
Yeh, I'm finally on the right side of the law
The right side of the law

Bad Consumer

There's someone holdin' up the line
Just tryin' to save one dime
Why don't you get yourself a life
And please stop wastin' my time
No I don't need a membership card
And I don't want your damn coupon book
I don't ever want you to call me on the phone
I just want you to leave me the hell alone
Yeh I'm a bad consumer
From the lower middle class
If you don't like the way I roll
You can go ahead and kiss my ass
'Cause I'm all through with being nice
If you don't say nothin'
Then you won't have to say it twice

Come on, October

Come on, come on October, please don't let me down
Come on October, don't let me down
I'm so tired of standin' around
Underneath a burning sun
Bring on the stormy weather
We're all waitin' for the rain to come
It's been six ways from Sunday
Once in a blue moon
The boys in the grange are doin' a rain dance
You can't bring it on too soon
Tell me how we gonna raise our children
How we gonna keep the faith
When there ain't nothin' but dust in the wells
Nothin' but tire tracks cross the lake
Come on, come on October, please don't let me down
Come on October, don't let me down

Georgia, Bold and Black

Georgia, bold and black

I love the color of your skin

I like the way that you walked right into my life

Georgia, bold and black

I didn't mean to say it quite like that

Now I'm asking you to please come on back to me

Georgia, bold and black

I'm not trying to win a fight

It's not a matter of who is wrong or who is right

Sorry, Sweetheart

Are you waiting for the show to start?

Sorry sweetheart but it's not on today

Everybody has made other plans

That's the way it stands

I hope that you'll be okay

I hear the hue and cry of many voices

Time to pay the price for our poor choices

Down at the circus there's a three ring tent

And the star attraction gives it away for free

There's a ruckus in the rookery

But let it be, it's more of the same to me

I hear the hue and cry of many voices

Time to pay the price for our poor choices

Trophy Shelf

She had 'em and she wanted you to know
Put 'em on display everywhere she'd go
Wasn't shy, didn't keep 'em to herself
Wanted you to admire that trophy shelf
She didn't keep 'em long in the dark
And might just bust 'em out on a lark
Spent a fair amount of time crowded together
Close confined in suede or leather
They seemed to have a mind of their own
Couldn't bear to be left all alone
Like a two for one overnight sensation
Trending right now in some far-flung nation

Cherry Aurora

There's no future in death, I tell ya
It ain't even called a coffin no more
They used to pickle you in formaldehyde
And paint you up like a whore
Then close the lid on a beautiful Cherry Aurora
And carry you out the door
Close the eyes and put a smile on his face
Even tho' he met with a terrible fate
Who cares if there was beauty on the inside
As long as the corpse looks great
Then close the lid on a beautiful Cherry Aurora
And carry him out the door
Put me in a backless suit
And some o' them upward-bending shoes
I'd look real good in a cashmere sweater
Tell me, how could I die any better than that ?
Then close the lid on a beautiful Cherry Aurora
And carry me out the door

Billet-Doux for You

When the buttonbox and the violin play

Everybody's dancing or tappin' their feet

Half the girls are pregnant

And the weather can't be beat

I was down to the marketplace to get a bite to eat

It was on the 8th day in the month of May

Oh sweet victory, everyone so deshabille

I was spittin' seeds, reclining on the lawn

But I'm the one you cast your eyes upon

Never mind what all your girlfriends say

This could be your lucky day

When I get back to my little shack

I hope to dream of you

And if by the grace of God I wake up in the morn'

I'm gonna write you a billet-doux

Deadman's Hill

When my bride is a widow

Then everything will be alright

I'll be the evil spirit

Come and visit her in the night

She don't care if I live or die

And that's a natural fact

You know a broken heart would hurt me

Worse than a heart attack

Gonna buy me some canned heat

With my last dollar bill

Gonna take me a walk

Up on Deadman's Hill

King of Cuba

My patience was wearing thin
Waiting for the show to begin
When is the wisdom of the subject
Ever smarter than the king?
And you were so close to being phenomenal
But you just couldn't close the deal
When your sordid world is so colorful
Why would you want to make it real?
You said you could make me the king of Cuba
If I would just leave you alone
You did not cry when we said goodbye
You were already gone as far as I could see
And Cupid is still shooting his arrows
But they just keep on missing me
Unrequited love is such a waste of time
So thank you for setting me free
Now I'm backing my Cadillac out of your alley
I do appreciate the offer of royalty
You said you could make me the king of Cuba
If I would just leave you alone

My Anodyne

Every time that I get drunk
I think it's all under control
But sooner than later I know
It's all gonna take its toll
I don't much like the company of strangers
I would rather just be alone
Got a jug o' wine, my anodyne
Waitin' on me back at home
I'm gonna take a little look around
Make sure the coast is clear
Have a little nip from a flask on my hip
And then ease on outta here

Last Laugh

I'm gonna wash my hands, gonna wash my feet

Gonna walk on down a different street

I'm gonna find my rhythm

I'm gonna find my groove

Believe me baby, it's time for me to make my move

You may think you got over on me

But you didn't get nothin' but my money

You can't take away my faith

You can't take away my past

Tell me now baby, who really got the last laugh?

Love to Do

What I really want our love to do
Is bring out the best in me and you
And when we get together
I will take you in my arms
Tell you 'bout all of your charms
Got to steady the hand, God speed the plow
Days fallin' down like dominoes now
I'm makin' headway, I'm takin' a stand
I got a love affair and a business plan
Maybe it's time to get off o' that stage
Start spendin' time with my piquant Page
Been a long time in them ofay bands
I got a love affair and a business plan
And when we get together
I will take you in my arms
Tell you 'bout all of your charms

Heat of July

A light enters the darkness
Bringing me back to reality
Wish I could find just a little bit more of me
Just a little bit more of me
What ever happened to the things we were promised?
What have we really got to lose?
Like the ballerina who danced her life away
Driven by the red shoes, driven by the red shoes
Could be heaven sent, could be time better spent
Maybe it's not for me to know the reason why
And I'm fallin' down in the heat of July
Fallin' down in the heat of July

Oh! Marisela

Oh Marisela, what the hell are ya doin' to me?

Oh Marisela, what the hell are ya doin' to me?

You put me down without a reason why

Oh Marisela, the way that you make me cry

Evanescent and argentine

Ultraviolet, radiating

Red for passion, desire and love

Blue for wisdom and faith

You like striking provocative poses

Bathed in a sensual light

I never know what you're up to

A Virgin Mary on the left, a calavera on the right

Justice Has Left the Building

I have no more need of reckless emotions
Like heartache and jubilation
And there doesn't seem to be a choice
Besides burial or cremation
After you kill my mortal flesh
There's nothing else that you can do
But my spirit will make itself busy
Visiting misfortune on you
And the woman who weeps the most
Seems to always grieve the least
The tears ignored by living husbands
Are useless to those deceased
It was there at the Midland Hotel
Where Rolls met Royce in 1904
That I remembered I was a soldier
Who fought in the Trojan war
Justice has left the building
That's how it appears to me
Someday all the pundits will say
That this was World War Three

Persona

Just knowing it would be there in the morning

Let her get to sleep at night

People only saw her when she wanted to appear

Saving up her muse and her solitude

And the same people who love you

Without knowing you

May hate you when they do

With just a modicum of talent

You can lose your self-doubt

Build up a fourth wall

And shut the people out

The only way she was gonna be someone

Was to be somebody else

She'd have to die before she met Mr. Right

It was the story of her life

But they could not kill her persona

Only the person that she used to be

B-Cup Beauty Queen

She woke up in a groove

But then she lost her touch

She was feelin' real smooth

Right before it got rough

She's a baby boomer

She's an early bloomer

Bonafide, certified

And holdin' a ticket to ride

So you take her for a ride in the countryside

To get her ready to go

You wanna give her the time

But she's still keeping all her kings in the back row

A B-cup beauty queen

With the best stems you ever seen

She'll be comin' 'round the mountain

With a diamond in between

Perihelion

Seven stabs of the dagger

The blood comes pouring down

Better tie up your belly, tie up your head

A lot of talk won't save you now

Hot chili pepper 'cross the virgin

See if you be truly possessed

Iwa Maman Brigitte

Won't be second-guessed

Days and seasons, perihelions

Cannot keep me from an unmarked grave

Throw my bones in the charnel house

Let my blessed soul be saved

Disorder Syndrome

They put her on Pradaxa
So she would not have a stroke
So she had another burger
With some fries and a Coke
They told her that Harvoni
"Would be just right for you
But don't you stop takin' it
'Til your doctor tells you to"
Trintellix that she took
Made a difference in her life
Now she thinks of suicide
Before she goes to sleep at night
With a magic bullet up there in the breech
And foria relief for the cleft of the peach
W.A.D.A. Told her that meldonium was wrong
Now she gets it in the mail
From Russia for a song

Finger in It

"I'm lucky to be alive,"
I whispered to the nurse
Robbed a hooker down on main street
She only had ten dollars in her purse
Hot-wired an old pickup truck
Threw it in reverse
Gotta get outta this town quick
Before things get any worse
Skip the romance, cut to the chase
Find a woman that you hate
And just give her your place
And when your soul begins to spring a leak
If a bullet hole starts to bleed
Just put a finger in it, put a finger in it

I Predicted Pain

I looked up in the sky and I predicted rain

I looked into my heart and I predicted pain

I was broke and I was hungry but I never did complain

Put my trust in the queen of diamonds

Rachel was her name

When death looks in the window

And the crow sits in the tree

Better keep your bones together

'cause they're just dyin' to be free

You know I've seen it all but I never felt a thing

'til you finally closed my eyes

And brought me peace again

Halfway to First

Good things come in all kinds of packages
Just met one I'd love to unwrap
I busted my moves and quenched our thirst
But I couldn't get halfway to first
The picture of beauty I'm taking in
The hot pursuit of a carnal sin
At first I was blessed but now I am cursed
'Cause I couldn't get halfway to first
Turn you on like a light, get you off like a shot
I'd give you more than you've ever got
Nothing much scares me but I fear the worst
I can't even get halfway to first

Today in the Park

Today in the park all the birds were singing

Imagine if they could hear the thoughts in my head

Oh the way things might have been

If we had never met

They talk about you every once in awhile

They say that you're doing well

I'm drawing the devil on the wall again

Going through my personal hell

The world stands still and the air moves around

The fire goes up and the rain falls down

Take my past for what it's worth

And give it back to Mother Earth

Just Like Buck

My mind is snappin' like a whip
I'm gettin' ready for a whole 'nother trip
Somebody bring me my medicine, man
Gonna take care of business as fast as I can
I'm gonna have my favorite meal
And play me one last gig
Then just lay on down and die in my sleep
Like ol' Buck Owens did
Late to the party 'cause I got a late start
Couldn't quit the party of the second part
Did 'bout everything but I never did no time
Always took my gin with a slice o' lime
I'm gonna have my favorite meal
And play me one last gig
Then just lay on down and die in my sleep
Like ol' Buck Owens did

Nothing is Sacred

I will save you from tragedy if I can
But I cannot save you from yourself
When everything seems perfect then somebody's fakin'
When everything's normal then nothing is sacred
The pursuit of wealth and domestic bliss
I am not burdened by any of this
And you tried so hard to be perfectly honest
But I preferred sweet little lies
Following trends, who knows where it ends
We only know how it begins
Following trends, who knows where it ends
We only know how it begins

Roaring 20's

The roaring 20's was a whole lotta fun

The 18th amendment didn't bother me none

Business was brisk, I tell you the truth

Drinkin' beer and smokin' stogies just like ol' Babe Ruth

Shoulda seen what I saw at the Vaudeville show

Two little flappers sittin' in the front row

We had a good time back at the hotel suite

That chicken and daughter combo can't be beat

We used to live in a brownstone out in Brooklyn

Mama always singin' whenever she was cookin'

Then she'd say we got to purge the evil from this place

And she would make us bow our heads and say grace

Cupid Sneaks In

McNary went a-fightin' o'er the waves yes he did
They brought him back home in a box with a lid
When he sat up and said hi to his mum one last time
She took hold of her heart there and then
And then she died
Took hold of her heart there and then and she died
The old man and the young widow
Got on best that they could
The both of them livin' in the same neighborhood
O'er time 'twas no secret they 'ere fond of each other
Now McNary's young widow has become his mother
McNary's young widow has become his mother
Cupid sneaks in with a sly little grin
And afore you know it he's got you ag'in
Cupid sneaks in with a sly little grin
And afore you know it you're in love ag'in
Afore you know it you're in love ag'in

She Came in Peace

She came in peace

She gave her love

Then she broke my heart

Now she's all that I'm thinking of

I try to learn, I try to listen

Another puzzle with a couple of pieces missin'

It's a blessing and it's a curse

God almighty I don't know which one is worse

It's the unwritten rule without a doubt

If you wanna profit then you gotta put out

She came in peace, she gave her love

Then she broke my heart

Now she's all I'm thinking of

First to Fall

Oh give me rest, gentle rain

Calm my nerves, quiet my brain

Hear the ticking clock and the humming fan

No, some things were not meant to understand

These are the moments that we're living for

Not just to live but be a part of it all

So where do we take it from here

And who will be the first to fall?

Just take it easy and make it true

Know where you are, know what you do

To stay too long or quit too soon

Which one is worse, I'm asking you

I couldn't move a mountain in a thousand years

But I can use my words and move you to tears

So where do we take it from here

And who will be the first to fall?

Take a Day

Once upon a time when there were no flowers
It was survival of the sweetest
Beckoning to, and promising you...
A fine line between poison and perfume
These days it's all for the predator
And nothing for the prey
After running around for so many years
It's time that I took a day
Like a black widow spider
I'm looking for a place to hide
'Cause the porch light still comes on at night
Even tho' there ain't nobody livin' inside
Now I'm setting my sights on the future
Rejecting the pleasures of the past
I'll never raise a white flag even tho'
The hero seldom lives to see the credits roll

Twenty-Second Century

I heard what you said, I read what you wrote
About millions of dead men still castin' a vote
The season is changing from summer to fall
You're crying for help but I can't take the call
No one ever talks about the 22nd century at all
No one ever talks about the 22nd century at all
I like some things when they're happening
But I don't miss them when they're gone
The kind of things that happen now and then
When everything else has gone wrong
No one ever talks about the 22nd century at all
No one ever talks about the 22nd century at all
No I don't look back in wistfulness
And I don't look back with regret
What more is there to wish for
When the best of passion is spent

Guardian Angel

Remember when you were just an ingénue
and I was a young buck chasin' after you
Well, I've been blown by the wind and rocked by the waves
Now the space between us gets smaller every day
And it's good to know I've got a place to go
when the heat comes pressing down
I'm still living (who knows for how long)
on the dark side of this town
There's a guardian angel watching over us
on the dawn of a new day
A guardian angel looking out for us yet
Good things are coming our way

The Potter's Field

The Catholic wagon rolls on by

Wheels grinding the Earth

Nary a drop of rain in sight

Everything's dyin' of thirst

The grave digger straightens the tombstones

Underneath the summer heat

A woodpecker up in the alder tree

Tappin' a steady beat

For the vultures that live by the side of the road

It's a hard time finding a meal

And the old wooden crosses without any names

Falling down in The Potter's Field

I work in the garden, go to the market

Keep company with angels and ghosts

All these dreams of ordin'ry things

The things that I miss the most

For the vultures that live by the side of the road

It's a hard time finding a meal

And the old wooden crosses without any names

Falling down in The Potter's Field

La Perla

The businesses shutter one by one
But the dogs of La Perla are still on the run
Drinkin' cervezas as calm as can be
And no ships make a wave on the wide open sea
Walking the silent streets all alone
While beautiful people in beautiful homes
Shelter in place from the specter of death
And Mother Nature does catch her breath
It's time to stop kissin' the cheek
Time to stop shakin' the hand
Time to start keeping some distance
It's time for the Thai wai, man

CPSIA information can be obtained
at www.ICGtesting.com
Printed in the USA
LVHW080146160421
684699LV00014B/386